THOMAS ATTWOOD
EASY PROGRESSIVE LESSONS
FOUR SONATINAS
Edited by Richard Jones

GW00371158

THE ASSOCIATED BOARD OF
THE ROYAL SCHOOLS OF MUSIC

Thomas Attwood (1763–1838) was an English organist and composer who held a number of appointments in the royal patronage. In his early years he studied in Naples and in Vienna, where he took lessons from Mozart, who said of him: 'He partakes more of my style than any scholar I ever had; and I predict that he will prove a sound musician.'

Most of his compositions were for the stage or the church, but he wrote a number of instrumental works, including these pedagogic sonatinas which were first published *c*.1795. In the first edition of *Easy Progressive Lessons Fingered for Young Beginners on the PianoForte or Harpsichord* there were no marks of expression or dynamics, and these have been added by the present editor. Attwood's meticulous fingering has not always been followed, and in several places the editor has filled in harmonies (shown by smaller-size note-heads).

Sonatina no.1 in G

ATTWOOD

*B.14, L.H., 3rd note: b in original edition.
†B.16, L.H., 5th note: crotchet in original edition.

RONDO
Allegro

Sonatina no. 2 in C

8

MINUETTO
Moderato

*B.15, L.H., 3rd beat: ♩♪ in original.

RONDO
Allegretto

Sonatina no. 3 in F

*bar 13, L.H.: minim in original, but cf. b.21.

Sonatina no.4 in D

[THEME AND VARIATIONS]

[Theme]
[**Andante**]

Variation 1

*B.36, L.H., 7th note: d' in source.

Variation 2

Variation 3

*b. 83, L.H. 2nd beat: crotchet rest in source, but cf. bar 87.

14

Variation 4: Minore

Variation 5: Majore

[**Allegretto**]

*B.92, R.H., 2nd beat: crotchet rest in source, but cf. b.76. †Bb.133 & 149, R.H., 3rd note: e″♮ in source.

[Variation 6]: alla Marcia

Maestoso

16

[Variation 7]

Allegro alla Tedesca